Raven's Eye

Raven's Eye

Terry Lee Spahan

authorHOUSE®

AuthorHouse™
1663 Liberty Drive
Bloomington, IN 47403
www.authorhouse.com
Phone: 1-800-839-8640

Published by AuthorHouse 11/10/2012

ISBN: 978-1-4772-9092-7 (sc)
ISBN: 978-1-4772-9091-0 (e)

Library of Congress Control Number: 2012921733

Any people depicted in stock imagery provided by Thinkstock are models, and such images are being used for illustrative purposes only.
Certain stock imagery © Thinkstock.

This book is printed on acid-free paper.

Contents

Dedication

For my best friend, my mother Joan Spahan, and my hero, my father Sammy Spahan. Without them, I would not have the strength and foundation to follow my dreams and explore the unknown.

Introduction

I sit contemplating what is and was and will be, as my mind flies away with uncontrolled thoughts that consume my very soul. I realize with this day and all days our minds are the doom to our happiness. Because this is the very curse from which I run.

These issues set forth brought into this world of chaos. Make the nightmares real and you are dammed by your own self destruction.

All because of these images put in the mind that is sedentary of work, that this house, which holds the soul is dwelling on things that cannot be changed, because the story told isn't your own, but one that dragged you in and held you down, by your own will, or lack there of.

This curse of never being full always searching for that knowledge not yet learned, or to meet the people whose stories are never told. I am not the author but the ears, which capture this tale and transform it to history by rebirth.

So set before you is observations of that which I have witness or been a part of. These people have entered my life and impressed in my mind beyond the norm and because of this, these thoughts have leaked on to paper in order to escape my prison, which is my mind.

So enjoy these ramblings.

The darkest part of my soul

Circles we are bound
Chains and locks hold fast
On the ground

Aches and pains run so deep
My blood feeds on the grief I keep

The eagle flies a round to feed
Trapped a animal I will be
My blood is what he seeks
My heart is what he keeps

The wind blows, the eagle drifts
On the waves of the weak
Soaring above all below
From the heaven we seek

I am bound, here to earth
Soul as black as the ravens wing
I hear a call in the night

So weak, so torn
Deaf to the call
Blind to the light

Dawn becomes dusk
My soul stirs, my heart beats
Night becomes day
As I wake from the darkest part of my soul

Ocean Green

Half of me is gone
Abandoned
Drifting searching
Wondering the days of endless nights

Questioning, purpose
Looking in from beyond
Your smile and laughter
Fill my ears, and make my tears

Peace you have found
But not for me
Eternal war I fight

A battle lost
But a war to win
What is love again?
Death inside, my heart gone black

Sea of green haunting me
Beneath this ocean
Dolphins swim

Whispered words
Knives cut to severe cords
Bound to me your pain cuts deep

Saved your soul
Of that unknown

Lift me up, draw me near
Make me hear
The whispered words
I scream I shout
Let me out

You are free
But here I roam

Eyes of new

Captured my heart you did
Sweet words, caresses of fire,
words etched in my mind
Eyes of new

Night captured lost in time
So free
Mask off,
Touched my soul
Behind the curtain, act one

Knees weak
Heart beats
Breath taken with the wind

Old sorrow found
Tricks play
Expectations and doubt
Clouds fill the air

Ice melting, tears falling
Mind wondering
Why drink the world away
Thoughts of new, act two

New is old in a different way
Expectations far and wide
Disappointment and sorrow
Act three, is it me

Build my wall, close this door
Empty faces, lost in rhyme
Seconds become days
What, could have been is gone

A lone in steel waters
Nestled in this cloud
Spirits bound are yet unfound . . . .
Curtains closes, no act four

Drumming told

pools of grey
true and blue
Still waters do seep

Heart beating beneath my feet
Drums beat
Fires burn
Bodies swirl in the flame

Souls two
Brought to one
Prediction told
Left unsaid

This quite obsession
Yearned and crept
Unconscious thought
Fought the urge

Yet the drums
Hypnotic beat
Told the story

In this fire true to see,
desire
Set free

Canada dream

Awaken
Body floating, turning
Voices all around
Foreign words filled my ears

Is it real
Awake, but asleep
Light so bright
In shape of a window

Looking in this window found
Spinning round are voices
Of different sound
Unknown words to my ear
I am home in this foreign land

Bound to this ground
Blood has pasted
Generations, roamed
Are they calling me home?

Eagles, floating drifting
Water flowing over beavers sleeping
Brother bear searching
Peace at last
Silence

Except one thought
Not my own
My Father spoke
His night mirrored mine
My sleep last night was full of voices
Calling me, my body floating, spinning

Separated by land
He once roamed, in a land not my own
Ancient ones
Called to us
To come home

Pebble in the water

Every thing and nothing
Behind this mask
Of self reform
Is a demon of its own

Covered
Within these mountains
Water falls cut deep
My tears seep my life cheap

Drowning in this body
Captured in this pool
Clouds of darkness
Brought gloom

Leads me as death greets me
Life needs me no more
I am but dust on the shore

Dry falls
etched in rock
is a path beyond a pool

Prey

The shadow crosses the raven's eye
Darkness sets in , the night begins
In the light of day

Sleeping is the tiger
Waiting to pounce
Eaten raw flesh
Heart still pounding

Drums of the heart
Stirs the wind
Carnivore's eyes bleed blaze red

Green grass
Dries to the wind
Serpents creep on the bladed floor
Mice hide from being prey

The raven sits
Capturing the sky
Reflecting its wings of blue

Shadows cross the raven's eye

Renaissance

Time has stopped
But a moment
as life spins around
Each minute a treasure

Change is what you hate'
But we are future and past
Brought together as one

Your eyes
A window to your soul
Holds no secrets, words unspoken
Said within one glimpse

Held fast by desire
Lighting strikes as we touch
Fire burns within us beyond our control
We are but one flesh

Spirits of past haunt my mind
Centuries back comes forth
You to me and I to you
Souls of old we both have been

Sent back, death greets me
Body numb, water falling
Your voice calling me home

Brought together by one
Time is but a question
Unanswered is the rhyme . . . . .

Picket fences

A part of nature yearns in me
Wanting to drift and explore
Untamed lands, no more
roaming the land
tied and bound
barbed wire all round
Drifting
tumble weed blows

Trees to wind
Brings these cries in the night
as the roots dig deeper in

Over rocks clear and cold
water flows
Caressing that unknown
Endless shore

Flames scorch and blacken earth
Skeletons of Trees rooted in sand
Stand fast is that fence
dividing the land
fading is the hooves
on the ground

Enemy

Lost in this path of darkness
Trying to find the light
Blind leading blind
Weak leading strong

I am bound in myself
A shadow with in
Behind this darkness
A light but creeps

I walked this path
I've crossed a bridge
Burned so deep,
The water beneath bare feet

Embedded is my sorrow
Impurities
Eat at my soul

Each day I pray
Yet I sway
I try so hard to do what's right
But human nature
Tares my might

Challenged,
Journey endless
invisible

to myself ill be
my own worse enemy

Eternal struggle

Your blood, my blood, there blood
Not our own
Conceived not by choice

A world of darkness
Not white but red
Skin to skin
Same blood fills these veins
Your dark I am white

A cancer fills the mind
Chemically induced
A battle within
So tired so worn

Years of pain
Self hatred the blame
Inhibited
Inhibitions all the same
Chemically induced, uncertain pain

Driving the death
Behind the cop
Suicide entices the mind

Again this blood so thick
Eternity sums a path of color
Rainbows seen through this rain
Spun quickly white remains

War Drum

Red
Fuse short
Temperature rises
Lighting flashes, thunder sounds

Glazed over reflecting the fire inside
Earth shake
Body quakes
Rapid beat felt at feet

Reality
Is cold
Frosted is my belief

Human nature takes hold
Split tongues
The snake speaks
A politician he be

Touched is the life
Lived and held
Not religion bound
By beliefs no one else seeks

Truth be told
Circles round
As earth is turning
Hearts beat
War is sought

Internally held
To forever seek
What is at our feet

Like a war drum my hearts beats
Reflecting the fire inside
Water is the gold we all hold
Depleting is this land

Human nature stands true
Always searching never found

Morals

Lost before spoken
Intuition sound
Held by this diamond

Lawless
Nothings scared
Only the score

A ring goes round
Found a curse
Sparkling in the light

Blank slate hidden deep
Dark pools
Reflects deceit

Forked tongue
Splits the words
Held as true

Media based
Bullies dealt
Crimson sunflowers
Spread the pedals

White bleeds red
flower cut
pedals fall

wilted in deceit

Retreat

Arm full of energy
Held to the heart
Wind blows eating
At the dirt

The grass dances up the hill
As if waves on a ocean green
Dust on the ground circles fast

Chills frost
Deep inside the needles prick
Dried the wet on this land
Hawks drift on the tides

Swaying softly around
Pray found
Straight dive swoop up

Hidden in the saddle
Six they stand
Held fast ears perked
Blending with the land

Noise breaks
Silence lost
Once hooves beat
In retreat

Sprit child

Your eyes see
Beyond years of infancy
Your old soul speaks
But you young body fights it capture be
Stuck in this body of a baby weeps
Dependant on those for keep
You yell and scream
Someone open up your ears

Searching your eyes be
All around you see
The world
Unable to express
Locked in a prison wee

As winters pass
and spring renew, your body grows

you watch the creatures and
rivers flow the beavers be
hours you see the turning of each new leaf

the world evolves
as does your people
choices made you question
logic

no lies told
truth quite bold
hoping they will see

the eyes you say
are the windows
for all that be

in these windows
life is seen
sickness and death

every window is open
you just need the key
spirit child
what is it that you see?

Little boy Blu

Sleep my child, may your dreams be sweet.
May you fly, and run faster then the wind.
As your creative mind fills with more adventure
And when you wake may your dreams blossom
Sleep my child rest your growing body
The innocence on your face, brings a smile to mine

Your breathing brings peace to my soul
As your lids cover your deep brown eyes, the light brings
your
Perfection for all to see
Seeing you smile even as you sleep
my heart missed a beat
Sleep my child
May your dreams be sweet

Looking at you fills my heart with pride
Sleep my child
Each breath you take reminds me of rebirth
Of the future next

Thirsty

Caught
Hungry
Thirsty
Wind calling

Either which way to shore

Mountains look cold to touch
Crisp and bright
A leaf crumbled to the ground

Thoughts are pools
Of clear deep water
Gone dark to the light
swimming in shallow water

dust floating free
lifting to the beat
from the pounding of the feet

as dry as this dust
snow falls to the ground
trying to settle

smooth as silk
rough as sand

breeze blows by
whispering a name
know to be my own
inside my mind
craves sleep

Unique is what I am

Struggles within
Fighting to be free
What is on the outside hides the in

Outside looking in
Inside looking out
A mask I wear

Beauty is but skin deep
It is the soul I seek
Eyes of dark, lips so fierce
What can I pierce??

Hallow on the outside
Hard on the inside
A shell I'll be

I look in the mirror
a stranger's looking back at me.
What was and what is
Begging for you to see
I am here, I am me, I need you

Struggles within fighting to be free
What is on the outside
Hides the in
Beauty is but skin deep I wish to cover every inch

I am but a shadow of my creation
I am lost, struggling to exist
Unique is fighting to be me

Your puppet?

Can you see my pain?
Deep in my soul
Do you feel the sadness?
Beyond repair

Behind this smile
Do you see a frown?
In my eyes that shine
From the tears falling down

When I speak
Do you hear my sorrow?
Behind the laughter
Do you hear my cry?

Can you see?
Can you hear?
Looking at me what do you see?

A puppet for the world to be . . . .

The edge I walk . . . .

Chemicals cloud my mind
Right and wrong I know no more
Everything and nothing, but all this pain
Regrets and depts. spent and lent

Hidden behind this mask
Pretense and suspense
a shadow covers my soul
Thorns puncturing my heart

Fear leads me
Death greets me
Life needs me no more

The pain so deep
My tears seep, my life cheap
The edge I walk
Chemicals cloud my mind
What of yesterday or tomorrow
Is but mine to say?
Regrets and debts all mine to pay.

Hidden behind this blame
Yours not mine
Is mine not yours
As chemicals cloud the mind.
The edge I walk . . . .

Sub Conscience sleep

Darkness
Breath is heard
A steady beat of heart
Rings
Old mind searches
Eyes glazed
Drifts about in the night
Present lost in unknown
Places and faces
Know to the conscience
Hidden in
Numbness is illusion
Between awake and sleep
Waiting to run
But tethered to the ground
Circles remain etched in the light
Loneliness burns deep
Hallowed with in
A shell remains
Behind this ravens eyes

Secrets

Shared is your secret
Deep down , blacken soul
Search through that darkness
Within no light

No hope
Twisting turning
Cries
Hidden below

A sea held
Seeping out your dam
Of regret
Fears of lost tomorrows
And yesterdays

Aged in darkness
White flesh
Ill to the light

free from this grasp
That you hold
Tied by barbed wire

My heart
Bleeding blue
Of internal pain

Yet beyond this shadow
I hold no light
Justice weighed
The scales tilted

Secrets kept

Sappling

Mother Nature takes hold
Planted that seed
A sapling growing from a weed
A flower Ill never be

Watered and feed
Knowledge led
A hot house I won't be

Taught from worlds lessons
Surrounded me of life
Music feed my veins
As my feet danced off beat

Crossed the country
Dusted by that wind
Planted firmly your tree
Does bend,

Forward bound
Clocks tick, chimes count
Hours pass
Youth gone, bones crack
Wind blows, snow falls

Seeds planted, saplings grow
Generations next
stories left untold
But your legend lives on

As customs fall
Life passed on

You are my gold
From which I am spun

Mother Earth

Wind blowing
Air lost,
Mind twisting
Howling a coyote calls

Whistling in the wind
Burning inside
Nothing is or does

Leaves falling, rustling about
Chill calls to the bones
Expressed in flame that burns

Rain falls
Exiting fears
Time passes

Beyond the gift
Thunder struck
Medal melting
molding to its form

rolling waves of fire
scorch the blacken
land remains

hear me
fear what is beyond
the known

I am the source
of life to which you live

Gypsy soul

Pain deep inside
Reminding me of the sea tearing at the shore
Each peace washing away
As the sunsets

I run to new horizon
Miles back, the mirror reflects
Reality sets in
Journeys no end

Life senseless
Risk taken, untainted in my crime
A moment thought, time bought
For what I don't know

Wondering the earth
Trying to fill that void
That's hidden deep within

Endless towns, Highway bound
Cookie cutters and sidewalks
Representing each town

As this wind blows by
Silence screams
Emptiness still found

Ice melts water falls
Earth parts
Shore to shore
endless bound

In my mind

lost
Beyond the shadows
mind captured
tortured
Soul empty

Unknown purpose
Outside the realm
A yearning
A place unknown

Bound
Invisible to the naked eye
Held fast by mind
Unable to let go

Demons
Feed by grief
Propelled by deceit

planted
Grounded by roots
Cuts run deep
Sap seeps

Longing to be without
Touch
cold and dark

Hidden in a world with in a world
Captured in my mind

New found sorrow

Ghost images haunt the mind
Past caught in a present time
Pictures burned, etched within

Captured and refined
Lost moment, lost time
Unable to rewind

Nightmares bought life to sleep
Tainted and scorned
Runs so deep,
these veins Run cold

The coyote calls
Answered back to this song
A chorus echo's in the night

Ravens fly all about
Taking the eyes and the light
Ghost images haunt the mind
Past caught in a present time . . .

Diamond of the rough

Wasteful of the light
Excrete from my pores the gift of my soul
Seeping is my blood

Each gift is my soul dying
Black and burned
Charred as a coal
Harded by the vultures

Blacken soot
Burnt in a stove
To heat the cold
Hearts of restless souls

Stealing energy
Sought by seekers
Deprived from love

Depleted
Batteries run cold
Windows frost
As does those blacken hearts

Who seek material objects
To fill that dark void
With the cost of life
Ever more.

Thorns, thistles, knives

I crave that grass on the other side
Dare I cross that divide?

Each blade reflecting the light
Tempting me for a bite!
Clouds cross over
Sun light fades

A trophy
Don't touch, don't speak
Or even see!
The trophy is mine you just leave1

Demons hidden with in
The owl called in the night
Bringing me much insight
As he calls the snake speaks
With forked tongue, the web is spun

Every day is a mountain
Every step an imprint
A path formed from past to present

A puzzle
Pieces fall
My reflection
Screamed out in a dream
Your shadow held my soul

Free my soul

Take this pain away from me
Take this pain away

Take this heart and make it pure
Take this soul and make it whole

hear the angles calling me
with open arms and helping hand
and my love ones near full of fear

take this pain away from me
Take this pain away

Say goodbye
Rest your hearts
I promise you, I'll see you soon
They are here to set me free

Take this pain away from me
Take this pain away

Reminisce, laugh and cry
Then say goodbye
Ill fly away on open wing

I hear your cries and see your pain
Watching me in agony
I try so hard to be your strength
But this pain is killing me

take this pain
Let me fly away with them
Leaving behind this empty core
This pain will be no more . . . . take this pain
away from me

Drift wood

I am but a stick in the sand
washed away by the raging water
white caps dancing over the rocks
broken but not beaten I drift alone

smashing against the banks
brought up on the shore
dried in the sand a tree no more

rain it pours
like tears on a floor
taking with it me once more

rocking in the waves
drifting shore to shore
cradled like a new born

piled high holding back
pressure built and weakness found
out all is bound
cutting deep into the sand
making mud through out the land

drift wood follows evermore
piled up on some random shore
gathered up on this beach

set to torch
the flame does burn
once was wood now I am
ash drifting on the wind
I drift alone

Dancing

Our bodies sway
To the music of our hearts
One rhyme against time

The answer being
Age and redemption
Expectations and guilt

My mind questions
What my heart feels
Your eyes speak,
Words unspoken
But truth be know, I am alone

Timid I am
Of what is and not
Burnt and spent

Empty space,
Together bound
Words no end, or begin

Anything you wanted was the answer
Nothing is what I got,
Damaged beyond repair
Bodies sway to hearts beat

Look at you girl fills the air

Blood bath

Tainted is this land
All touched by man
When nations meet
Cultures deplete

Stained
Ripped apart
At the heart

Blood bound no families
Found
Generations and nations
Split and torn

New reborn and old remain
Blood mixes
New is formed

Cultures split and destroyed
Lost a tongue and arts
Sacrificed in religion

Tainted is this land
Stained by blood
Of nations past

Never to be found

Printed in the United States
By Bookmasters